Anne Jordan

The Christmas Hero

A story from
The-Front-of-Beyond

DayOne

© Day One Publications 2022

First printed 2022

ISBN 978-1-84625-735-3

Published by Day One Publications
Ryelands Road, Leominster, HR6 8NZ

TEL 01568 613 740 FAX 01568 611 473

email—sales@dayone.co.uk

UK web site—www.dayone.co.uk

All rights reserved

No part of this publication may be reproduced, or stored in a retrieval system, or transmitted, in any form or by any means, mechanical, electronic, photocopying, recording or otherwise, without the prior permission of Day One Publications.

Internal design by **documen**

Cover design by **Kathryn Chedgzoy**

Printed by **4edge**

Dedication

This book is dedicated to Home for Good, a
Christian charity with a Biblical mandate to care
for vulnerable children.
Home for Good is dedicated to finding a home for
every child who needs one.
See homeforgood.org.uk

For those children who are adopted or
fostered, this story is especially for you.

Chapter one

The Christmas decorations were now up. Stefan thought the whole house looked good. He had been the one in the family to put the star on the top of the Christmas tree this year. He had tried hard to get the star straight, but it just flopped to one side. He didn't mind too much. Maybe it had been born that way. Maybe there was a factory that made wonky Christmas stars. Mor and Malc had both tried to straighten it. His brother Nick had had a go too. But the star still refused to budge, so it stayed wonky.

Anyway, the star made him feel good about himself as he was sometimes wonky too.

He had been told he had something called epilepsy, which made his body shake and fall down, but it didn't bother him. He and his brother Nick were fostered, but that didn't bother Stefan either.

His carers whom he lived with were called Morag and Malcolm. When Stefan had been little, he couldn't say their names properly. His little mouth had managed Mor for Morag and Malc for Malcolm, and the names stuck.

He called Malc's mother Mamo because he had wanted a grandma. Mor said that Mamo was another name for grandma in the Scottish language. Mor knew lots of clever things. So Mamo it was, and Stefan loved her very much from that day onward.

CHAPTER ONE

Mor fussed a lot. He didn't need it—after all, he was eight—but she made great dinners, so that made up for it. It was only him she fussed over, not Nick. Nick was eleven. Nick told him one day that double figures were special. Nick liked numbers. Nick could count to six hundred and fifty-five in fives. For the past two weeks, Nick had been telling him how many dinners and how many puddings they would have before Christmas Day

They had now arrived at dinner number fourteen and pudding number fourteen. It was a Saturday, and it was just him, Nick and Mor at home as Malc had gone to see Mamo. Malc went to see Mamo most Saturdays. He did any odd jobs around the house that might be needed.

Dinner and pudding number fourteen took no time to eat. They were just as good as dinner and pudding number thirteen. Mor had been quiet during dinner. Usually she chatted away about this thing and that; she was never quiet. Every now and then she started to say something, then stopped. Stefan wondered if she was getting a cold as she kept blowing her nose. When they finished eating, they collected the dirty dishes. It was Nick's turn to wash them today and Stefan's job to dry them. Mor always put them away as she was tall enough to reach the high shelf in the kitchen cupboards.

After she had finished, she turned to them and spoke. 'Now you two go into the lounge and wait for me there. I'm just nipping out to the shed for a moment to get my walking shoes. Sit still until I come back.'

She wasn't smiling.

They did as they were told. Was something wrong? Not much went wrong in The-Front-of-Beyond, the village where they lived.

When he had been six, Stefan was told about The-Front-of-Beyond from Malc, who said that as it was getting near to Christmas it was just the right time to have a really special bedtime story. Malc said to listen carefully, so he did.

'This is the story of The-Front-of-Beyond and how it came into being. A long time ago, an old gentleman who lived across the sea arrived in London. He told everyone he met in the streets that he had just had a wonderful holiday in The-Front-of-Beyond. A lot of people laughed at him and said he had had too much fine ale, but some people believed him.

'The man then went to see the king of England in his palace and told the king all about The-Front-of-Beyond. The king believed him and then told everyone in the palace that there is a wonderful place called The-Front-of-Beyond. He said that everyone who lived there ate chocolate biscuits for breakfast and drank purple lemonade before they went to bed. The king said that was what the gentleman from across the sea had told him and how sensible it was too. It was much better than eating the boring stuff like everyone else ate and drank.

'Everyone in the palace cheered the king because it was the polite thing to do.'

Stefan had laughed then. Malc had laughed too. And that had made him laugh even more. When they had finished laughing, Malc said, 'Now it is time for you to

CHAPTER ONE

go to sleep as it is a long story. I will tell you the rest tomorrow night.'

At bedtime the next night, Malc carried on with the story.

'Then the king went outside to the palace gate and told all the people he saw to go to The-Front-of-Beyond for their holidays. After that, he brought out a new map of Great Britain. He put The-Front-of-Beyond next to The-Back-of-Beyond at the top of Scotland. This was because there was a lot of space there. And so it was that The-Front-of-Beyond was born.'

Stefan had been proud that he lived in a place that the king himself had thought special.

He was now thinking back to how special that Christmas had been. He had been given his first watch. He looked at it now for a few minutes. It kept good time. He hoped he would have the watch forever.

He was still thinking about the watch when the lounge door opened and Mor came in. She sat down next to them.

'Now listen up, both of you. There's a problem with the giants.'

Stefan, like everyone who lived in The-Front-of-Beyond, knew about the giants. It was the only thing that spoiled the village. The giants lived on a large hill known as Giant's Hill which overlooked The-Front-of-Beyond and were different from other giants. They were lazy and silent. All they ever did was lie on the grass, year in and year out. Stefan and many other Beyonders wondered if the giants were asleep forever.

The villagers took turns to keep an eye on the giants. Summer and winter, they watched carefully. The giants seemed to prefer warm sunny days, especially in summer when a lot of Beyonders were doing outside things.

So far nothing bad had happened. In the end, the Beyonders stopped bothering themselves about them. After all, some places had worse things like volcanoes and rivers that flooded. Stefan, like everyone else, had stopped thinking about them too. But now Mor said there was a problem with the giants. Maybe they were planning a secret attack. Maybe they were getting organised.

He felt his heart begin to beat faster. It only did that when it was his turn to read aloud in his class at school. He felt a tear wet his eyelashes. He didn't want to cry. Crying was for babies. Instead he opened his eyes wide and coughed hard. The cough made Nick jump. Stefan guessed Nick was thinking the same as him.

'You know how the giants have always looked the same,' said Mor. 'Well, in the past few weeks they have got longer. Look, lads, it might be that they are on the move. Even the IBs are worried. Someone might get hurt or—well, worse. There's a meeting this afternoon at the village hall to discuss it. Everyone has to go. Malc is still at Mamo's house. They will come later.'

Stefan knew a lot about the IBs. They were the Important Beyonders who were in charge of The-Front-of-Beyond.

The IBs were five important women and five important men. The women were the doctor, Doctor Be-well, the head teacher of the school, Miss Sit-up-straight, and the post office lady, Mrs Tie-string. The lady who ran the village clothes shop was called Miss Sharp-needle. Mrs Spinning-top was her sister, and she owned the toy shop.

CHAPTER ONE

The men of the IBs were the vicar, the Reverend Hard-pew, the dentist, Mr Spit-it-out, the bank manager, Mr Ready-cash, the librarian, Mr Right-page, and the fruit and vegetable man, Mr Wind-sprout.

(There was no butcher's shop in The-Front-of-Beyond because it had burnt down. It had been run by Miss Sit-up-straight's father, who had since gone to live by the sea and now sold fish. Now a butcher's van came around the village three times a week instead.)

Oh yes, Stefan knew all the IBs, and just like Mor, he always said to them 'Good morning' or 'Good afternoon' when he saw them in the street. He always put on his best smile too.

He tried to do that now to see if it made him feel better. It didn't. Mor must have noticed the smile because she patted him on the head.

'I know it's a worry for us all. And you were hoping to make pizza this afternoon too, but never mind. You can make it sometime this week, I promise. And as usual, there will be tea and cake afterwards at the end of the meeting. I'm taking some of my mince pies.'

Beyonder meetings always ended with cake. All Beyonders liked cake, whether they were happy or sad.

Stefan did feel disappointed about the pizza, but then he was feeling disappointed with a lot of things. It was winter, and it was supposed to snow in winter. It always did, but this year there had been no snow. It had been bright, sunny and frosty, the kind of weather grown-ups liked.

He had to admit it was nice to see the sun. It made him smile and was better than rain. He had gone out to play when he could. Then it had been very cold at night and he had woken up to spiky icicles on his bedroom windows. It looked very pretty, if you liked that sort of thing, but it was boring compared with snow. He was longing for snow.

Stefan wanted to try out his new sledge. His old one had become too small for him, and he had got a new one for his birthday in November. That morning he had opened his curtains and looked out hopefully, but alas, no snow. At least a meeting at the village hall would be a way of passing the time.

So what if the giants were getting longer. Maybe they would get even longer and really thin and then disappear. They did that sometimes anyway, disappear that is. Maybe they would disappear all together? Perhaps it wasn't a problem after all.

Suddenly a dreadful thought came into Stefan's mind. Were they getting longer because it was only two weeks before Christmas? Were they planning to get thin enough to slide down everyone's chimneys? Thin enough to steal all the presents on Christmas morning before anyone was awake? That would be really bad.

Christmas in The-Front-of-Beyond was always great fun. A huge number of parcels that had the wrong address would arrive at The-Back-of-Beyond. The postman had nowhere else to send them. There were so many that The-Back-of-Beyond postman would send those that were left over to The-Front-of-Beyond's post lady, Mrs Tie-string.

No one knew what was in the parcels. That was the most exciting thing of all.

Mamo had got a scooter last year from the parcels. She had been so excited with it that she had whizzed around the garden ten times without stopping. A toddler down the road had received a large Zimmer frame which he had laid down and spent a happy few hours jumping in and out of.

A lady Beyonder had received a do-it-yourself kit complete with hammer and nails. She loved it and made chairs to sell at the village Boxing Day festival. A bald middle-aged Beyonder had received an orange hair dye kit and as a result went into the wig business making orange wigs for those who wanted one. Stefan wondered if any Beyonders would be wearing them at the meeting. He would have to be careful not to laugh. But then, this wasn't a day for laughing.

This was very serious indeed. Would anyone in The-Front-of-Beyond have any Christmas presents this year? He tried to picture it, just empty spaces around the Christmas tree.

It wasn't good.

Chapter two

Stefan and Nick put their coats on as they had been told to and set off with Mor towards the village hall.

On the way, Stefan looked at his watch. They had been a bit late leaving the house. Mor had been fussing around the kitchen to find a tin big enough to put all the mince pies into. Eventually they found one, and Stefan agreed to carry it.

They were getting near to the village hall now. Stefan could see that many Beyonders were jostling and crowding the narrow doorway to get inside. He felt a bit nervous. He didn't really like crowds. They often had too many tall people in them. When they arrived, he was ushered through the door first in front of Nick. He knew Mor wanted him to get warm as quickly as possible. More fussing, but he was glad of it today as it was cold.

'Right,' said Mor, 'when we get in, I want us to sit near the front. I don't want to miss anything.'

'Yes, Mor.'

Stefan knew Mor was a bit deaf, but what could he do? The hall was filling up very quickly, and he had to take the mince pies to the cake table first. Fortunately, he spotted a number of ladies, all wearing bright orange aprons, collecting cake donations. He handed his tin over, then jumped up in the air to see if he could spot any spare seats. There were only odd spaces here and there.

Chapter Two

'Can't see any spaces for us all together,' said Stefan. Nick nodded in agreement. He had been looking over some of the heads in front of him. Nick was quite a bit taller than Stefan was.

'No, it looks as though we will have to sit at the back. Pity,' replied Mor. That would never do—oh no. Stefan was going to get a seat for the three of them if he died doing so.

'Right, follow me,' said Stefan. Quick as a flash, he darted to the side of the hall, calling out 'Excuse me' in an urgent voice. Kind Beyonders parted and let him through the crowd. He turned at the side of the wall to face the front and continued running, calling out 'Excuse me' all the time. He could hear Mor's quick breaths behind him and knew she was following him. He heard her whisper, 'Stefan, come back.' But he chose to ignore her. He assumed Nick was following behind.

He arrived at the front out of breath but triumphant. He looked along the first row. It was full of Beyonders he didn't know. No one was speaking and everyone looked serious. Then a thought came into his mind. He remembered a game he had played at school called Chinese Whispers. He took a deep breath, bent down and whispered something in the ear of the Beyonder at the beginning of the row. Then he said, 'Pass it on.' The surprised Beyonder did so. Very soon the message came to the very last person at the end of the row.

Suddenly, everyone on the front row got up and moved to the back of the room, leaving the front row completely empty. Mor was amazed!

'What did you say to them?' she whispered, sitting down on the middle seat in the front row.

Stefan sat down next to her and smiled to himself. His plan had worked. Then Nick sat down.

'I told the man at the end of the row that Malc said there is woodworm in the front row chairs and they could break any moment!'

Stefan knew about woodworm. He had heard Malc tell Mamo there was woodworm in her sideboard when they had gone together to visit her one Saturday. Later he had asked Malc what woodworm was. Malc had said that the worms ate things made of wood. Sometimes the things they ate would drop to pieces. Malc had looked very serious when he had talked about the nasty worms and what bad things they could do. Stefan tried his best to look serious now.

'You said that?' frowned Mor. 'That was telling lies. Now go and apologise to every person who moved for us.'

Stefan felt his face go hot. A single tear came into one eye and trickled down one cheek. He had only wanted to make sure Mor could hear, but in his heart he knew she was right.

Jumping to his feet, he ran to the back of the room. One by one, he told everyone in the back row that he had made it all up. Some Beyonders said he had been brave to tell the truth, some just scowled at him, but it was done. He arrived back very out of breath and sat down. He was just in time too as the IBs were now walking onto the stage in front of them. They then sat down.

Stefan watched as Mr Ready-cash stood up and raised his hand. It was a signal for everyone to stop talking.

Everyone went quiet. The meeting was about to begin.

Chapter three

'Ladies and gentlemen, residents of The-Front-of-Beyond ...'

Stefan sat up straight. You did that when Mr Ready-cash began to speak. Stefan wished, however, that it had been someone else speaking. Mr Ready-cash was a boring old windbag who liked the sound of his own voice.

The other IBs were not boring. Yes, his teacher did talk quite a bit, but she wasn't boring. She told wonderful stories. His favourite story was about a man called Nelson who at Cape Trafalgar saved Britain from being invaded by Napoleon. When he heard his teacher say the last words of Nelson—'England expects that every man will do his duty'—he cheered out loud. Everyone in the class laughed, and Stefan joined in and laughed too. When he heard that Nelson had been only five feet and four inches tall, he sat up very straight and proud. One day he would be like Nelson and do something brave. He would be a hero.

His teacher had also read a story to them about a man called David. The story was from something called the Bible.

He had liked the story as David had killed a man who was as big as a giant. David, who was only young and small, hadn't been afraid of the giant man who was threatening to kill lots of people. David had killed the giant with some small stones and a sling. Stefan thought that was a brave thing to do.

Half an hour later, Mr Ready-cash was still speaking. Stefan was beginning to feel sleepy. His eyes kept on closing. He tried blinking, but that made him feel funny. Suddenly, the door at the back of the hall banged open. Someone must have come in. A voice spoke loudly.

'Ooo, cake. Is it a party?'

Stefan recognised Mamo's voice immediately. She must have arrived with Malc. Mamo was always late for things. She had no idea about time. Chances were Malc would have had to wait for Mamo to put her best hat on. She would never go anywhere without wearing it. Stefan looked sideways at Mor. She had gone very red in the face.

'Don't look round. It's rude to stare.'

Stefan did as he was told. He really wanted to look, but he loved Mor too much to do something she wouldn't want. He hoped there would be seats for Malc and Mamo to sit on at the back.

Some Beyonders began to laugh. Stefan didn't like that. Mamo was a good person. She could kick a ball a long way. He couldn't imagine Mr Ready-cash kicking a ball. He would miss the ball as he was always walking with his nose in the air, as he was doing now, and worst of all he'd been talking for at least five whole minutes.

Suddenly Mr Ready-cash stopped speaking and coughed into the air above him. Then he moved his head downwards and looked at everybody. After a few moments of silence, he began to speak again, only in a much louder voice.

Chapter Three

'Fellow Beyonders, it's getting nearer to Christmas, and the parcels will be coming soon. Great sorrows could befall us.'

Mr Ready-cash's voice was so loud it made Stefan jump.

'The giants are getting longer, good people of The-Front-of-Beyond. It is possible they could descend down our chimneys and abscond with the copious presents we receive before we awaken on Christmas Day ...'

Stefan nudged Mor.

'What's he on about?' he whispered.

'He means the giants could get down our chimneys and steal our presents.'

Stefan nodded his head. No presents. Presents were the main thing about Christmas. No presents.

It wasn't good, not one bit.

'... and the other danger,' Mr Ready-cash continued, 'is the Boxing Day tossing of the Christmas tree competition. Just suppose the giants make away with our Christmas trees.'

This time Stefan knew exactly what Mr Ready-cash was talking about. The tossing of the Christmas tree competition was huge fun and part of the festival. On Boxing Day every Beyonder would take down all the decorations off their own tree and then tie the tree up very tightly with string. Everyone met together with their trees in a large field behind the school. Each family would choose one of its members to be the Beyonder who was to toss their tree. All tossing persons would then line up at the start of the race.

They would run with their trees to the count of fifty, stop and then throw their tree as far as they could. The winner, whose tree landed the farthest, would then be given a prize of Mr Spit-it-out's extra-white toothpaste. Everyone would cheer and then go to the village hall for hot chocolate and sticky honey cake, which was a great favourite of everyone who lived in The-Front-of-Beyond. In the evening there would be fireworks.

All the Christmas trees would be gathered up, and everyone was given one to take home. You didn't always get the one you had owned before, but no one minded that. Once you got home, you would decorate the tree that was now yours. The trees never came to any harm and were as good as new. Everyone who lived in The-Front-of-Beyond loved Boxing Day. Stefan tried to picture his house without a Christmas tree. It wasn't good, not one bit.

Stefan heard lots of murmurings behind him. It was clear many Beyonders were very worried. The thought of their Christmas trees being stolen was terrible indeed.

Mr Ready-cash held up his hand. Everyone became quiet once more.

'Something has to be done. I propose we attack these giants soon. I have a plan, and it's a good one. Every able-bodied man will be needed. Are you ready for the fight, men? It will mean taking time off work. Will you sacrifice a few days' work for The-Front-of-Beyond?'

Stefan heard lots of yeses behind him. He felt proud. Lots of men including Malc worked at the local Front-of-Beyond biscuit factory. It was a great job as everyone loved making the biscuits, which were the best in Scotland. Even people in England bought them.

Mr Ready-cash had now moved to the edge of the stage.

Chapter Three

'Well done, men. The attack will take place a week from Monday. This will give us time to get some tents from England. We will set up camp on the Sunday evening. Make sure you eat well during the weekend. Have lots of cake. You will need all the energy you can get,' continued Mr. Ready-cash. 'We can do it, Beyonders. This could be our finest hour. Miss Sit-up-straight has agreed to close the school just in case there is trouble. Mothers, you need to stay in your homes with your children. Do not go out until you hear the all-clear. Do you all understand?'

Stefan looked at Mor. He saw her smile and nod. He wondered if all the mothers in the village hall were nodding too. He couldn't resist looking around. It was then that he spotted Malc standing at the back next to Mamo, who was sitting down.

As he looked, Malc began to move towards the front of the hall. Malc wasn't smiling. Whatever was the matter?

'Wait! I have something to say,' Malc shouted.

Stefan couldn't take his eyes off Malc as he walked nearer to where Stefan was sitting. The village hall became quiet row by row as Malc got nearer and nearer to the front.

'Mor, it's Malc,' Stefan said. Why was she staring straight ahead of her, Stefan wondered? Had she seen a ghost?

'Mor, look, it's Malc. He's walking straight past us. Why is he going to the stage?'

Stefan noticed Mor's face go red. He had seen that look once before when Malc had got cross with Mr Right-page in the library about something. Just about everyone in the place had heard him. Mor had been with them. She had grabbed Malc's arm and hurried him outside and then said a word he didn't know. He remembered it now, the word was trackless.

Stefan wondered if Malc was going to be trackless now. Mor would certainly tell him off when they got home. He looked at Mr Ready-cash, who by now had sat down. Mr Ready-cash didn't look happy.

Malc was now facing everyone. He began to speak. 'Fellow Beyonders.'

Stefan smiled at that bit; at least Malc wasn't being trackless now. 'I want to say a big thank you to Mr. Ready-cash for thinking up a plan for getting rid of the giants, but it won't work.'

This time there was no cheering. Stefan noticed that Mr. Ready-cash's face had gone a strange shade of purple.

'It won't work because we don't know what weapons the giants have. We have no proper weapons. Our cricket bats and spades are not enough. It needs one person to sneak on them to have a look. We must have the same weapons as they have to fight them with. If not, we will lose.'

Stefan knew Malc was right.

No proper weapons.

It wasn't good.

'I am prepared to go alone at daybreak to find out what weapons they have, then report back to the camp,' continued Malc.

At this, Stefan held his breath. He had just had a horrible thought. He wanted to run onto the stage and grab Malc's arm, but didn't dare. It was no use though, as Malc was still speaking.

Chapter three

'I can then send a message with a runner to our friends in The-Back-of-Beyond. I am sure they will get us weapons in time for our planned attack later on. We must not try to get any weapons before the day of the attack. The giants may see us and guess what we are planning to do.'

Everyone began to cheer except for Mr Ready-cash, who had gone even purplier.

Stefan didn't cheer either.

It wasn't good. He knew why.

Only he—Stefan—could be the one to go. He was small enough, just like Nelson, to be the hero. He was small enough not to be seen. Malc was too big to be a hero. Stefan knew the giants would see Malc a mile off. Then all would be lost. Only Stefan was small enough to see what weapons the giants had hidden. He would be able to sneak up and hide behind big rocks and in small spaces.

He and no one else in The-Front-of-Beyond could beat the giants. But how was it to be done? He needed a plan of his own.

Chapter four

Stefan couldn't sleep. Everyone had kept coming to him and saying how brave Malc was and had patted him on the shoulder and given him cake to eat. He had eaten a lot of cake in the village hall and now had tummy ache.

His mind was busy too. He had to have a plan, but it had to be simple, something a small boy could do. He looked at the clock on the table by his bed. It had stopped. It was always stopping. Clocks—they were the boss in his life. Everything he did was to do with what time it was. Everything began with him waking up in the morning. He stared at the clock. He needed time to think. If only time would stop.

After a while of hard thinking, an idea began to grow slowly in his head. Yes, it just might work. He would ask Mor for a new clock, one with an alarm on it. An alarm that would wake him up early before anyone else was awake. That was the most important thing he needed to make his plan work.

It was good.

He could sleep now.

Stefan woke the next morning with his question already worked out. His mind had come up with it when he was asleep! He was bursting to ask it all the way through

Chapter Four

breakfast. At last, with one last spoonful of porridge he was able to say it.

'Mor, may I have a new clock, one with an alarm? Please,' he added.

'Well, I know your old one keeps stopping, but why one with an alarm?'

'It's because I can then wake up in time for school.'

He was telling lies again, and just as before, he felt his face go hot. He bent his head and scraped the last bits of porridge in his bowl onto his spoon. He then swallowed it. He could say no more, but how was he to get a clock?

'Trying to be good for Christmas then? Let's leave it until after Christmas. You never know what parcels you might get.'

'Yes, but Mor ...' He stopped speaking. He just couldn't think of an answer. He had to have an alarm clock. He had a whole week to think about how to get one. He thought about it all day Sunday, but nothing came into his head. The same happened on Monday and Tuesday.

By Wednesday he was so worried he couldn't concentrate on his school work. His teacher noticed and asked him if he was alright. He said he had a headache, which was true. His teacher said he could go home if he wanted. Stefan said he couldn't as Mor went to Mamo's house on Wednesdays.

Suddenly, a thought came in to his mind. Maybe Mamo would have an alarm clock. So he changed his mind and said that he felt worse and that Mor could be contacted at Mamo's house.

It all happened very quickly, and Stefan found himself at Mamo's house in no time at all.

When they got there, Mor told him to lie down on the settee. Then she put a rug around his knees. He groaned a bit about her fussing. But there was one good thing about it. He could see all around the room. Sadly, there wasn't an alarm clock anywhere. There were plenty of ornaments and photos and pictures of flowers and dogs.

Mamo liked dogs of all sorts of shapes and sizes. Maybe, just maybe, she had an alarm clock somewhere else in the house. How should he ask her? Then he had an idea. He sat up straight.

'Mamo, did Popo have an alarm clock with his trains?'

Popo, Mamo's second husband who had recently died, had set his model trains to go at certain times during the day. Stefan loved how Popo would say, 'It's now time for the morning milk train.' He would look at his watch and count down the seconds, and off it went. He missed Popo very much.

Stefan could see that Mamo was thinking about Popo too as she got a handkerchief out of her cardigan sleeve and said 'Oh, Popo!' She did that a lot. Each time she said it, she would blow her nose very hard. Then she would put her handkerchief away and say, 'Now that's enough.' She did the same now. Then she looked at Stefan, grinned and spoke.'Nay, laddie, it ain't a clock. It was a bacon sandwich with the eight-thirty from Glasgow!'

Stefan did his best not to laugh. He loved Mamo, even though she said strange things sometimes.

'You're not on about alarm clocks again, are you. Now just lay down, close your eyes and try not to speak,' said Mor.

'Mor ...'

Chapter Four

'Now then, no more talking,' said Mor, wagging her finger at him.

It was no good protesting, so Stefan lay down and closed his eyes.

In a way he was happy doing this as he really did have a headache. He could hear Mamo and Mor talking, but he didn't pay much attention to what they were saying.

Eventually he heard Mor say something about how it was time they went. He opened his eyes to hear Mor saying that Malc would pick them up tomorrow after work. He had no idea what that meant.

'Time to go home, young man, and it's an early bedtime for you tonight,' said Mor.

Stefan didn't really care about what time he went to bed. If his plan failed, all would be lost. He knew for sure that he was only small enough to see what weapons the giants had. He had to stop Malc from going to look for them and then getting hurt or even worse. It was awful just thinking about it.

It wasn't good. It was really bad.

However, he was glad to go to bed. Maybe he would be able to think of something the next day.

Stefan woke early the next morning. It took him just a few seconds to remember it was Thursday. His headache had gone and he felt fine. He got out of bed and was just about to make his way to the bathroom when he heard Mor call outside his bedroom door. 'Stay where you are, our Stefan. No school for you today.'

'But Mor, I feel fine. The headache's gone.'

'No, you might be going down with something. Can't have you poorly for Christmas,' she said, coming in to his bedroom.

'But Mor ...'

'No buts. You're staying in bed. I'll make you some porridge, then it's sleep for you.'

It was no use arguing with Mor. Hopefully, if he stayed at home today, he could go back to school tomorrow. Then he could ask his teacher if she had an alarm clock he could borrow.

Mor tucked him in and went downstairs. A few minutes later, she came back with a bowl of porridge on a tray. Next to it was a glass of milk.

'Now sit up. I want to see it all gone.'

She put the tray in front of him.

Stefan did as he was told.

'Right, snuggle down and I'll come back later.'

Stefan did as he was told and closed his eyes. He heard Mor close the bedroom door and go downstairs. As soon as she was gone, he sat up again.

It was then he heard the front door open and close again. Who could it be?

Chapter five

'What are you doing at home?' Stefan recognised Mor's voice as it floated up the stairs.

'Boiler's gone wrong. We got sent home.'

It was Nick. He had come home. Stefan knew about the school boiler. It was old and had a habit of going wrong during winter. The building would go cold quickly and the whole school would be sent home. Sometimes it was ages before it happened again, but sometimes it would happen a few times in a term.

'That stupid boiler. Now I've got the two of you at home.'

'Is Stefan off then?'

'In bed, so don't make a noise.'

Stefan smiled to himself. He knew for certain Nick would come and see him.

Stefan counted the footsteps on the stairs as Nick came up. Six more steps to Stefan's room and Nick would be opening his bedroom door. It was always six. Sure enough, Nick was in his room on the seventh footstep and tossing his school bag on Stefan's bed.

'Mor fussing again,' said Nick trying his best to be as brotherly as possible.

'Yep, but never mind that. Nick, can you keep a secret?' asked Stefan.

'Guess so, but you have to make me promise just in case.'

They each knew about the Beyonder promise. You had to spit on your hand and then rub the spit on your face. You then had to say, 'Beyonder do, Beyonder fie. If I split, I will die.'

'Right, together then,' said Stefan.

Stefan got out of bed and stood opposite Nick.

They both spit on their own right hands, then rubbed it on their own faces. Together they said the promise.

'Beyonder do, Beyonder fie. If I split, I will die.'

Stefan then got back into bed. Nick sat down in a chair next to Stefan's bed.

'Pull your chair up. I need to whisper as Mor might hear.'

Nick did as he was told. Stefan began.

'It's about the giants. You know what Malc said at the meeting. It won't work.'

'The weapons part and him saying he would go.'

'Oh, you did listen then?' said Stefan.

'I did at that bit. I mean, it was our Malc they were cheering.'

Stefan was about to say 'You were only there for the cake,' but decided against it. He really needed Nick's help.

'It won't work.'

'It will. He's Malc. He's big and strong.'

'That's why it won't work,' said Stefan, banging his hand on the bedclothes.

'What do you mean?' asked Nick.

'He's too big. Think about it. The giants will see him, and they might get him before he even sees the weapons.'

CHAPTER FIVE

'No, they won't.'

'They might do. It needs someone small to creep up the mountain. You know, hide behind those big rocks and just peep over them when the giants are not looking,' said Stefan.

'Who do you mean?' replied Nick. 'It was only Malc who said he would go. No one else said they would. Anyway, there isn't anyone small enough. Beyonder men are big and ...'

Stefan was now grinning from ear to ear.

'What are you grinning about?' demanded Nick.

'It's me, don't you see? I'm the only one who is small enough to go.'

'You,' said Nick. His voice had become louder in surprise.

'Shush, Mor will hear. Keep your voice down. Anyway, Nelson wasn't tall,' said Stefan.

'Nelson, who's he?'

'You know, Horatio Nelson, history, that battle on a ship.'

'But that was a long time ago, and ships don't come here,' said Nick.

'I know that. Look, I have an idea. I plan to get up early on the morning of the attack before Malc and everyone else does at the camp. Then I'll climb the mountain to see what weapons the giants have, then get back and report to the camp when they wake up.'

'It won't work,' said Nick decidedly.

'Why?'

'Because of Mor. She won't let you.'

'She won't know. Listen, that alarm clock I was talking about. I really need it,' continued Stefan. 'I plan to have a dummy run the day before the attack—get up early and try it out.'

'How do you mean?' said Nick.'Well, I need to get up before its light, run to Giant's Hill and wait until the sun comes up, then hide for a few minutes. I need to know what time to set the clock for to get it just right.'

'Then after the dummy run you'll come back home.'

'Yes, and then get back into bed as though nothing has happened.'

'Might work.'

'It has to. The thing is, I need your help. Can you get me an alarm clock? I'm stuck in this bed, might be for days, knowing Mor. Nick, I really need that clock.'

'I know where there is one—shush a minute. I think I just heard Mor's footsteps on the stairs.'

'Nick, is that you in Stefan's bedroom?'

Stefan dived under the bedclothes at the sound of Mor's voice. He counted Nick's quick sudden footsteps as he fled his room.

Stefan knew what would happen next—Scotch broth at lunchtime and thick slices of bread with lots of butter on it. It was Mor's way of looking after him. That was exactly what happened. He knew the afternoon would be boring. He read for a bit of the time and then put his book down.

When he heard Mor hoovering downstairs, he knew it was safe to get out of bed. So he got up and stared out of the window. Then he dived quickly back into bed when he heard her come up the stairs. Eventually evening came, and Malc came home from the biscuit factory.

CHAPTER FIVE

Stefan was glad when Malc came up to see him later on after dinner. Malc didn't fuss like Mor. They played boxing together for a bit. Then they played a few board games. Eventually Malc said he would have to go as Mor would tell him off for 'overtiring the lad'.

'And just before I go,' said Malc, 'Mor and me have asked Mamo to come and live with us. She said she might do if the cat dies. I said we don't mind having the cat. Then she said it won't live much beyond spring. Not sure if that meant yes or no. Well, I'll try asking her again in a few weeks' time.'

Stefan grinned and nodded his head. Malc then said he would come back later to say goodnight. Then he left. After he had gone, Stefan thought about having Mamo living with them. He decided it was a good thing. Mamo was fun with or without the cat.

He then spent the rest of the evening reading a comic. At last he heard Nick's footsteps on the stairs coming up to bed. He counted the footsteps again to his door, and then Nick came in.

Nick was grinning as he came towards Stefan, who had now put his comic on the floor. Nick was clutching his stomach in a very peculiar way. He brought out an alarm clock from under his jumper.

Stefan gasped in delight.

'Told you I knew where there was one,' said Nick.

'Where did you get it?'

'Guess. Not too far away.' Nick grinned. 'The shed, you numpty.'

Stefan grinned at Mamo's favourite word, numpty. It meant someone who was stupid, but he and Nick had begun to use it in a friendly way when they wanted to tease each other.

'You've not been snooping among Mamo's things?' said Stefan. 'You're not supposed to do that.'

'It was just one look two days ago to see if any of Popo's train stuff was in the box, and I saw a clock among all sorts of boring things. So tonight I sneaked out after dinner and got it.'

'You've been in Mamo's cardboard box,' said Stefan in a slightly shocked voice.

Stefan knew all about the cardboard box. Mamo had a thing about collecting things from sales to bring home, all sorts of rubbish. Then she had begun to put her own pots and pans in cardboard boxes. She had told Malc to take it away.

Malc had brought the stuff home and put it in their shed. Then he had taken it back bit by bit and put it away in Mamo's cupboards. Then she would start all over again, putting her own stuff in cardboard boxes.

Lately it had got worse, and all sorts of strange things had gone into the box. The clock must have been one of them.

Stefan took hold of the clock. He made a silent promise as soon as he had finished with it that he would return it to the cardboard box in the shed. It wasn't stealing, it was just borrowing. No one would ever know.

'How do you set it then?' he said, looking at Nick once more.

Stefan knew Nick was clever with numbers.

'Easy. See the button that says alarm?' said Nick, sitting on the edge of Stefan's bed.

Chapter Five

Stefan looked to where Nick was pointing.

'Yes,' he replied.

'Well, you use that to move that really thin clock hand. Have a go,' said Nick.

Stefan did so. He grinned up at Nick. It was easy.

'If you want it to go off at, say, seven in the morning, you move that thin hand so it is on the seven. Then ...' Stefan watched as Nick told him the next thing to do.

After he finished the instructions, Nick said, 'Now try the whole lot.'

Stefan did so.

'How do you know about clocks?' asked Stefan.

He saw Nick's face go redder and redder.

'Not Mor and Malc's clock! Have you been playing about with their clock?' asked Stefan.

No answer.

Stefan guessed Nick had been up to something, but he would let it pass this time.

'So what time do you want to get up then?' Nick asked.

Stefan had to think about that. It was winter, and it was dark when he got up to go to school, which was about half past seven. The dummy run would be on Sunday morning. Everyone had a lie-in on Sundays.

'Do you think seven would do?' asked Stefan.

'Should do. Plenty of time for you to get dressed and sneak downstairs. Everyone has a lie-in on Sundays,' replied Nick.

'Brilliant,' said Stefan. 'Thanks, Nick, for the clock. You can have my piece of sticky honey cake on Boxing Day.'

Nick grinned, showing the one filling he had in the side of his mouth. Stefan knew sticky honey cake was just the best ever. Nick drooled over it every Christmas.

'I had better be off to bed now,' said Nick as he got up to go. 'See you in the morning.'

'And you,' replied Stefan.

Nick left, closing the door behind him.

After Nick had gone, Stefan put the alarm clock under his pillow. Then he picked up the comic he had been reading. He tried reading where he had got to, but the words in the comic kept on moving, and some kept disappearing then coming back. Try as he could, his eyes would not stay open.

The next thing he knew, he was dreaming about a piece of sticky honey cake that had grown clock hands and was running up a large Christmas tree! It was a nice sort of dream.

...

The next day, which was Friday, all the children in The-Front-of-Beyond found out that the school boiler was fixed. That meant Nick would be going back to school. Stefan wanted to go too. He managed to persuade Mor after lots of 'pleases' to let him go. He promised her he wouldn't run around too much.

Eventually she said yes. She sent him off in his thickest jumper and warm trousers and fleece-lined coat. She wrapped him in two thick scarves as he left the house. She also made him wear a very stupid hat because it covered his ears better than his favourite one. Halfway to school,

Chapter Five

he took the hat and one of the scarves off and stuffed them into his school bag. He arrived at school feeling very hot. He was glad to take the coat and the other scarf off.

The school day passed off as any other. Soon it was time to go home.

Saturday night and Sunday morning couldn't come fast enough for Stefan. He just knew his plan would work.

It was good. Just like Nelson.

On Friday, Stefan's dinner was as great as Mor always made it. He then spent the rest of the evening playing boy games with Nick, reading comics and eating some sweets Mamo had bought them. She had come round with them earlier as she had bought too many for herself.

Stefan gave her some of his comics to read as he thought it was a good thing to do. She smiled her lovely wrinkly smile. She looked at them for a while and then took them into the kitchen. He found them later on lying in a heap in the washing-up bowl.

Later on, she went to sleep in the chair. Mor and Malc said she could stay in the spare bedroom rather than go home.

Stefan kissed her goodnight before he went to bed himself. She woke up and told him to be a brave Scottish laddie. He liked that. It was good. Just like Nelson.

He woke early on Saturday morning feeling very excited. Only a few short hours and he would be back in bed and putting the alarm on for Sunday morning. He took the clock out from under his pillow and looked at it. It was just an ordinary clock which Mamo had owned and forgotten about. He put it back safely under his pillow.

He thought about Mamo again. He had no idea how old she was, but she had quite a few creases on her face. He had once asked her why her face had lines at the bottom of her nose. Mor had been there at the time and told him off for being cheeky. He didn't think he had been cheeky. It was just a question.

...

Saturday was a boring day. He ate breakfast, played outside for a bit then came in again. Then he had lunch. After lunch, he played outside again. Then he came back in again. He went to his bedroom and played with his cars. He kept on looking at his own bedside clock, the one that kept on stopping, wishing the hands would move faster. They didn't, but then it wasn't a very good clock.

Mor came upstairs later and told him it was his turn to eat the chocolate square from the advent calendar. He and Nick always took turns. She had the calendar with her. He opened the square, took the chocolate out and ate it.

It was good.

Soon after that, the sun began to set. Usually Stefan didn't much like the sun setting. Winter days in Scotland were short, sometimes getting dark after three in the afternoon. Today it was different. Not too long to wait until bed time. The evening meal would come next, maybe a story from Malc. To Stefan's relief, everything happened as he thought it would—good dinner, bedtime with a great story from Malc and a final goodnight from everyone.

Chapter Five

Nick was the last one Stefan saw. Before he closed Stefan's bedroom door, he looked back and mouthed the words 'Good luck.'

Stefan did a thumbs up sign in reply. Once Stefan was alone, he reached under his pillow for the alarm clock. Oh the relief when it was still there. Mor hadn't found it. His hands shook as he took the clock out. He turned it over and found the alarm button. He then moved the thin hand to the number seven on the clock face. The next thing was to set the alarm. How had Nick done it? He couldn't remember. He had to remember! He tried to imagine Nick showing him. He tried his hardest to remember Nick's words. Nothing came to his mind.

His eyes began to mist over. Some little tears began to fall down his cheeks. He wiped them away on his arm, but then more came. He couldn't stop them. The giants would ruin Christmas, and worse, Malc could get killed.

This wasn't good.

This was really bad.

The only thing he could do was to go downstairs and get Nick to show him again, but how could he do it? He was in the lounge with Mor and Malc and Mamo. They would wonder what was going on. Whatever was he to do?

Chapter six

*I*t was no good. He had to go down and talk to Nick. He got out of bed, opened his bedroom door and tiptoed down the stairs. He then walked the short distance towards the lounge door. He could hear Mor's, Malc's and Mamo's voices from where he was standing but couldn't understand what they were saying. He knew Nick would be there too as he had another hour before it was his bedtime. How was he to get his attention? Maybe Nick was reading a comic. Nick liked comics. Then he heard Malc laughing at something.

The laughing noise made Stefan think about when he and Nick told secrets to each other. One of the secrets Nick had told him had been about how a boy in Nick's class had kissed a girl behind a high wall. It made them both go 'yuck'. Later on they had both overheard a girl tell another girl the same story. The girls had giggled. 'Why do girls giggle?' he had asked Nick. Nick said that's what they did when they had secrcts.

Suddenly an idea came into his head. It might work. He opened the lounge door and ran inside, letting it bang and dashing to where Nick was sitting. Nick, as Stefan had thought, was reading a comic.

Mor looked up in surprise.

'What's the matter—are you feeling poorly?' she said.

Chapter Six

Stefan noticed she was sewing a button on one of Malc's shirts.

Malc looked up as well from reading his newspaper.

'Alright, lad?' he said.

'Yes, fine, I need to talk to Nick right now,' said Stefan. 'Nick, the secret,' he whispered, but loud enough so that Mor and Malc would hear.

He wanted them to hear so that they would think it had to do with Christmas.

'What?' said Nick.

'You remember, Nick, it's the time,' said Stefan, emphasizing the word time.

'Our Stefan, this is not ...'

Mor sounded cross.

It wasn't good.

'Now then, darling,' said Malc. 'It's the time of the year for secrets. I once pushed a pine cone down the back of the settee when I was a lad. I didn't tell anyone. Someone had told me it would bring good luck for the rest of the year. It was going to be my secret lucky charm. I forgot about it until Mamo found the broken bits later. It had been sat on too many times.'

'Alright, but make it quick. It's past your bedtime,' said Mor.

'Thanks,' said Stefan. He moved towards the lounge door, Nick following him.

'What are you on about?' asked Nick, once the door was closed.

'It's the clock. I can't remember the last bit.'

'What—oh, you mean the alarm clock?'

'Yes, the alarm clock,' said Stefan in an exasperated voice.

'Oh, alright then.'

Stefan raced up the stairs, followed by Nick fast on his heels. He opened his bedroom door and both of them went in. The clock was lying where he had left it on his pillow. Nick picked it up.

'Now look.'

Once more, Stefan watched as Nick showed him how to set the alarm.

Stefan had a go and this time got it right.

'Right, must go. Mor might moan at me,' said Nick.

'Thanks,' replied Stefan.

Nick got up and left the room, closing the door behind him.

After Nick was gone, Stefan put the clock under his pillow and climbed into bed. Nothing could stop the plan from working now.

It was good.

Just like Nelson.

...

The next thing Stefan knew was a loud ringing in his ears. At first he thought it was the school bell and that he was late for school. Then he realised the noise was coming from under his pillow. The alarm clock, of course—it must be seven o'clock. Then he remembered it was early Sunday morning, the day of the dummy run. He grabbed the clock from under the pillow and turned the alarm off. He threw the bedclothes off the bed and got dressed without bothering to have a wash. His adventure had begun.

Chapter Six

He opened his bedroom door, which was at the front of the house. Then very quietly, he tiptoed past Mor and Malc's bedroom, then past Nick's bedroom, which was at the back of the house, next to the bathroom. Then finally he passed the spare bedroom which was on the side of the house, where Mamo was staying for the night. Her door was slightly open, and he could hear her snoring.

He then made his way down the stairs to the hall. He unhooked his jacket from the coat rack near the door and put it on. He felt for the front door key, which was always on the hall table, and eventually found it. Very slowly, he placed the key in the lock and turned it. It opened the first time. He went through the open door and closed it carefully.

He turned to walk along the path. He began to walk towards the road, ignoring the strange feeling that was coming into his head. Maybe it was the cold air that was doing it. He walked a few more steps, but the strange feeling got stranger. He felt as if he was beginning to float away. Everything around him was a bit wobbly.

He felt himself falling backward. His body began to twitch. Slowly, blackness slid across his eyes like two doors closing next to each other, then, nothing ...

...

Some minutes later, Stefan opened his eyes and blinked them. Mor was bending over him. His head hurt a lot, and he felt cold all over. He felt sick too and very tired. All he wanted to do was sleep, but why was his bed so hard? Malc was standing next to Mor. That was strange too.

'Stefan, it's alright. Malc will carry you up to bed.'

Stefan stared as Mor's face went away and Malc's face came nearer. He felt Malc's arms pick him up. Stefan felt the air rushing at him. It did bad things to his stomach. Some sick came and oozed down his chest. He coughed, and from nowhere came a towel held by a hand. He looked at the hand and followed it up the arm to the face. It was Mamo.

He felt himself moving. The front door appeared and opened by itself. More sick came. A hand appeared again and wiped it away. Now he was climbing. He heard voices behind him, Mor and Nick and Mamo all saying things together. Then a door opened by itself and he was lowered down. He looked all around him. He was in his own bed. He looked up at the ceiling. A light was dancing by the window. It was too bright. It wasn't good. He closed his eyes and the light went away...

...

Sometime later, the sound of a door banging somewhere in the house woke Stefan up. He opened his eyes. He was in bed, and by the side of his bed sat Mor reading a magazine. She didn't usually do that when it was time to go to school.

'Feeling better now?' she said.

Stefan didn't know what to say. He couldn't remember being poorly.

'You've had a long sleep, best thing. Now don't worry, you usually bounce back quite quickly.'

Stefan had no idea what Mor was talking about.

'Now don't try and move while I get you a drink.'

That was easy. For some reason he didn't want to move. He felt very strange as if he was in a dream.

Chapter Six

Yes, a dream, he had been in a dream. He must find the dream again. The cow had been carrying him up a grassy hill ...

'Stefan, Stefan.'

Stefan heard his name. Why was the cow talking to him?

'Stefan, open your eyes. It's me.'

This time Stefan knew it wasn't the cow talking to him but his big brother Nick. He opened his eyes.

'Alright then?' asked Nick.

'Think so,' replied Stefan, taking in the size and shape of his brother, although he wasn't quite sure if he was alright or not.

'Do you know what happened to you?'

'Did something happen then?' asked Stefan, now feeling much more awake.

'Sure did. You had a fit,' replied Nick. Stefan didn't reply. He knew he sometimes had fits, but he hadn't had one for a long time. 'Bet you can't remember.'

'No,' replied Stefan.

'Can you remember anything?' asked Nick.

Stefan thought for a while. He was glad Nick didn't stare at him. Nick was good at not staring. He remembered going to bed and there was something he had to do. He thought a bit more. Yes, something about a clock. That was it, the clock, the alarm. Then it came to him, the dummy run.

'Got it,' he said.

'The clock and everything else,' said Nick.

Stefan nodded his answer.

'You must have got up alright, got dressed, gone outside and then had the fit,' said Nick triumphantly.

'I do remember feeling a bit funny.'

'It was Mamo who found you.'

'No, was it?' said Stefan.

'She must have woken up and for some reason gone outside,' said Nick. 'She found you sprawled on the path. Then she woke Mor and Malc up. Told them she had found you by the front door. And she was still in her pyjamas. And she hadn't got her slippers on.'

'What did Mor say?' asked Stefan.

'I couldn't believe it. You knows how she fusses?' replied Nick.

Stefan nodded.

'Well, she was different. She got Doctor Be-well to come, all calm-like. I didn't hear what they said as they closed your bedroom door. A few minutes later they came out together. I heard Mor say something about how you must have gone out because you were confused, then something about you always bouncing back quickly. Then Doctor Be-well said something about you being fine after a few hours or so.'

'Mor not making a fuss, that's new,' said Stefan.

'Odd.'

'You just can't tell with people who have a difficult name like Morag,' said Stefan.

'No.'

Stefan then went quiet with the sudden realisation that his plan hadn't worked.

It wasn't good.

It wouldn't have happened to Nelson.

'So, our Stefan, what are you going to do now? It's four o'clock in the afternoon,' said Nick.

'Just thinking about that. It's no good. I shall have to do it without the dummy run.'

CHAPTER SIX

'No, you can't do that. It's too risky,' said Nick.

'Yes, I know,' replied Stefan,' but I have to do it. I have to do it for Malc. Can't risk anything happening to him.'

'Look, you, this is dangerous. I mean, those giants might get you. What would I say to Mor and Malc if—well—you know?'

'You mean if I get killed?'

'Well, yes,' said Nick with a shake in his voice.

'Not going to think about it,' replied Stefan decidedly.

He yawned, feeling tired again.

'Look, Nick, before you go, can you do the clock for me?'

'Yes, but if you get kil ...'

'Just do the clock,' said Stefan.

'Alright, bu ...'

Stefan clamped his hand over Nick's mouth and handed him the clock. Nick took the clock and checked that the alarm was set. He then handed it back to Stefan. Stefan then put the clock under his pillow. Nick said no more but got up and quietly left the room, closing the door behind him.

Stefan closed his eyes again, but sleep didn't come. Nick had been right when he told him he could get killed. His heart began to beat a bit faster. He thought about his family and his school and The-Front-of-Beyond. He didn't want to leave any of it, but what was worse was being without Malc. Malc was big and kind and funny and helped people like Mamo.

Malc together with Mor had given him a nice home to live in and a brother too.

Malc did secrets.

Malc had to stay alive.

Malc was good.

Just like Nelson.

Stefan was now exhausted. All the thinking had given him a headache. He didn't hear Mor come up later with some food. He heard nothing until the sound of an alarm going off the next morning.

...

Stefan woke with a start. It took him only a minute to realise what day it was—the day he would sneak up on the giants and see what weapons they had. No time for second thoughts. He gulped back some spit that had come into his mouth and got up. He fumbled for his clothes in the dark and put them on. Like the last time, there was no time for a wash. Being clean wasn't important when there were giants to face.

Very quietly, he opened his bedroom door and tiptoed onto the landing. He closed his bedroom door and made his way once more to the top of the stairs. Very slowly, he put one foot onto the first step, then the other. So far so good. He continued down the stairs as quiet as a mouse. It was going well. Once in the hall, he sprang towards the front door in two large leaps. He found his coat and shoes and put them on.

The thick brown curtains that hung over the front door were closed. They were always closed early in winter months to stop any draughts from coming in. He searched for the key on the hall table. No luck.

He spread his fingers out towards the edges of the table. Then he felt every space there was on the table under the photograph of his grandparents and around

Chapter Six

the curved edges of a Christmas Cactus plant. The key definitely wasn't there. He could guess why. Mor had probably put it somewhere so that he wouldn't go outside again. He could just imagine her thinking that she'd better hide the key in case Stefan wanders off into the night.

The key could be anywhere. If he went searching the house, he risked being heard. He had to get out of the house, but how? Suddenly, he heard a faint creaking noise from upstairs. He stood very still and listened.

Silence.

He was just wondering if he could get to the lounge, open a window and climb out when he heard it again. Someone was coming down the stairs. Quick—he had to hide, the door curtain. He dived under it and stood very still. He listened as the quiet footsteps came nearer to the door. It was all going wrong again.

It wasn't good.

The steps were close to him now. Stefan took a deep breath. Was it Mor or Mamo? he wondered. He tried desperately hard to think of a reason why he was hiding under the hall curtain early in the morning. He knew Malc would be at the camp. If it was Mamo, then he might be able to say that he was bringing her cat who was very hungry and had turned up looking for her. If, however, it was Mor, then his luck was up.

Suddenly, the footsteps stopped on the other side of the curtain. Stefan heard a few rustling sounds. He held his breath and waited.

Which of them was it?

Chapter seven

'Stefan, it's me.'

'Nick, what th ...' said Stefan in a relieved voice.

'Shush, let me under the curtain. I've got the key, but don't speak,' whispered Nick.

Stefan did as he was told. He watched as Nick unlocked the door and then buried the key in the soil of the cactus plant. A shaft of light from a street lamp outside peeking through the window showed him that Nick was fully dressed with his coat and shoes on. That explained the rustling noise he had heard. Neither of them spoke. Nick then opened the door, and they both stepped outside. Nick closed the door very slowly, taking care not to bang it.

'Run, but don't make any noise,' whispered Nick. 'I'm coming too.'

'What!'

'There will be time for questions later. Just run.'

Stefan did as he was told, but he was determined not to let Nick go near the giants. His plan depended on only him doing it.

They ran together in the direction of the hill. If there had been some moonlight, then Stefan would have seen a small crack in the pavement. The moon, however, had deserted them both and hidden behind thin, eerily-shaped

CHAPTER SEVEN

clouds. There was no silver light to protect them. The street lights only shone a short distance in front of them.

Stefan tripped, catching his foot in the crack and falling awkwardly to the ground. It all happened so quickly that Nick wasn't able to save him. He stopped running and helped Stefan shuffle up to a garden wall. They both sat up with their backs to it, panting and breathing hard. Stefan felt hot and a bit dizzy. He said nothing to Nick about being dizzy, though. Nick was the first one to speak. 'Are you alright?'

'I think so, but my ankle hurts,' replied Stefan, rubbing it hard with his hand. 'Can't feel any broken bones, though.'

'Let's just sit for a minute.'

They sat in silence, getting their breath back. Eventually Stefan had recovered just enough to speak.

'Nick, about you ...' he began.

'Guess you want to know about the key?' interrupted Nick.

'Well, yes and—there are other things I need to sa ...'

'When I left you last night, I was determined to come too. I know you wouldn't have it, but I couldn't let you face it on your own, not after that fit. I felt bad about the dummy run. I should've come then.'

'Well, thanks, but ...' said Stefan.

'I'm not finished yet,' continued Nick. 'Last night I heard Mor tell Malc before he went out that she was going to hide the key in the plant so you couldn't get out. I was just coming out of the bathroom when I heard her say it. I waited after she had gone to bed, then sneaked downstairs and took it.'

49

'Thanks a lot, Nick, but you do know I can't let you come with me.'

'I've been thinking hard about it. How about you climb the hill and I stay down as a lookout just in case anything happens. If something does happen, I can run and get Malc at the camp.'

Stefan sat and thought for a while. There was sense in what Nick was saying.

'Alright then, but mind you keep to the plan.' His head had cleared, and he didn't want to waste any more time talking.

'You bet I will.'

Stefan began to get onto his feet, forgetting for a moment about his ankle. A sudden sharp pain stabbed his foot.

'Ouch,' he cried out, leaning on Nick, who had got up himself.

'Grab my arm and try running on your toes. It's not far now,' said Nick.

Stefan did so. It wasn't easy, and Stefan wasn't happy with the speed they were going, but at least it was forward and not backwards. His ankle hurt a lot, and he had to stop running and walk.

After a few painful steps, they passed the last house in the village. The last street light to lighten their way was now behind them. Open fields lay winter bare on both sides of the road. It was very quiet except for strange night animal noises. In Stefan's imagination, tall hedges which he felt rather than saw became places for monsters to hide behind. The sudden noise of a solitary croaking

Chapter seven

bird made him jump. He was glad now that Nick had decided to come with him.

They were now making their way slowly along the road which wound away from the village. A cat brushed its way against his legs. He felt its quick warmth. They had slowed down much more now, partly out of fear and partly because Stefan was finding even walking more difficult. The pain in his ankle was getting worse. He decided not to tell Nick.

Some clouds in the sky parted briefly, allowing the moon to light up the scene in front of them. Immediately they saw on one side of the road four rows of tents lined up in the centre of a field. Behind this was Giant's Hill, large, shadowy and mysterious. Then a moving cloud covered the moon, bringing darkness back with it. It was very dark now. Stefan shivered, not because he was cold or because they had arrived. He felt cold because of what he was about to do.

It was up to him now.

Chapter eight

The first thing they had to do was find the gap in the hedge which led on to the field where the camp was. Stefan had seen it many times before, but it was almost impossible to find it in the dark.

'Can't find the gap,' he whispered to Nick. 'What about if you go in front and feel your way along. Then tell me when you find it.'

His ankle was hurting much more, and he leaned on the hedge for support.

Nick did as he was told and moved in front. Stefan waited as Nick edged himself forward, feeling for the gap as he went.

Stefan knew that the hedge was very thick.

'Keep going, Nick, the hedge becomes thinner and it parts in the middle.'

'Found it,' said Nick.

'Good job,' replied Stefan.

Stefan crawled his way along the hedge to where he thought Nick was, accidently bumping in to him when he arrived. The bump made Nick slip on some mud.

'Sorry, Nick.'

'It's ok. Follow me through the gap.'

Nick went first and Stefan followed.

They both managed to squeeze through the gap.

Chapter eight

'I think it would be better for both of us to crawl now,' said Stefan. 'Can't risk being heard by anyone at the camp.'

'Good idea,' said Nick.

'We need to crawl along the hedge and then turn around at the bottom,' Stefan whispered. 'Then we follow the hedge along until we know we will be getting close to Thor's Head and Giant's Hill.'

They set off together.

The ground was hard and icy. The cold damp soaked into their knees, but neither spoke to each other. Onwards they crawled. It was a slow job. It was beginning to get a bit lighter now, making their journey easier. Stefan guessed it was nearly dawn. He had seen the dawn so many times on his way to school. The sun was lazy in winter. It didn't want to get up just like him.

By now the sun was just light enough for Stefan to see the hill which was a short distance in front of them.

'You hide here, Nick,' whispered Stefan, pointing to a clump of trees by the hedge where the ground dipped before rising again to Giant's Hill.

Nick nodded and did as he was told.

Stefan could just make out Thor's Head. Thor's Head was a collection of old stones arranged on one side of the hill in an oddly-shaped circle. From a distance, it looked as if the stones had faces. Mamo had told him all about what they really were and why they were there.

She said they were trolls who once upon a time were strange human beings. Thor was their leader. The trolls had come from Norway. Mamo said they had turned to stone in the sunlight thousands of years ago. Mamo had told him not to go near them.

At any other time, Stefan would have stayed away, but now he had no choice. They were the perfect place to hide behind.

Stefan took a deep breath and hobbled the best he could towards Thor's Head. His heart was beating very fast, and he was still feeling dizzy. The sun was now coming up behind the hill. It was getting brighter all the time.

He hid behind the biggest stone. Now and then he would dare to look around one side of the stone. Each time he looked, there was nothing to see. He wondered if the giants were hiding behind the other side of the hill. Maybe they were watching him, wondering who would make the first move. It was a scary thought. He was very glad that Nick was keeping an eye on him.

He was now feeling very cold. His hair was damp with sweat and now stuck to his forehead. His ankle hurt even more, and his tummy rumbled. He thought about the hot, filling porridge he would be eating for breakfast if he was at home. He wondered if Mor and Mamo had discovered that he and Nick were missing.

Stefan shook himself to get rid of the thought. He had to concentrate. The sun was now over the hill. Dark, high-up areas were being flooded with sunlight. A few birds were singing. The sun spread down quickly to where he was hiding and covered him with light.

Morning had arrived. This was it, the day he would face the giants. Stefan continued listening. Apart from the birds singing, there were no other sounds. Twice more, he looked around the stone he was hiding behind. As before,

Chapter eight

there was nothing to see. There was nothing for it. He would have to come out of hiding.

He remembered the story of David and Goliath. David hadn't been afraid of the giant man and had killed the giant with some small stones and a sling. Well, he didn't have a sling, but there were lots of stones lying on the ground. He bent down and grabbed three large ones that were closest to his feet. The sun was so bright now it was shining in his face. He rubbed his eyes, which were bleary with lack of sleep.

Then with one brave step, he came out from where he was hiding. Imagine the shock when in front of him was one giant longer than him lying on the ground. He could just see it, even though his eyes were very bleary.

He took the biggest stone out of his hand and with the other hand threw it hard against the giant. The stone bounced and rolled away! Stefan watched with amazement. Then he bent down. The giant did the same. Stefan then put one hand out. The giant did the same.

Suddenly he began to laugh. He laughed so much it began to hurt his stomach. He flopped down behind the stone and laughed some more. He now knew everything about the giants.

'Nick,' he called out at the top of his voice, 'come here.'

He was still laughing when Nick arrived, puffing and panting. He flopped next to his brother.

'Are you alright?' he asked. 'Is it some kind of laughing gas?'

'No, I'm fine,' said Stefan, trying to control his laughter. 'Just stand there, Nick.'

'Won't I be seen?'

'No, just do as I do. Throw this stone.' Nick did as he was told, but with his eyes closed. Stefan wondered if Nick still wasn't sure if there was gas around.

'Open your eyes, you numpty, and do it again.'

'Well, if you think it's alright.'

'Yes.'

Nick opened his eyes and threw another stone.

He too began to laugh. He had seen what Stefan had seen.

'Does that mean—?' asked Nick.

'Yes, it's the same for everyone,' replied Stefan. 'The giants are just our shadows. We have been frightened by our own shadows. There aren't any giants, never have been.'

It took a little while for Stefan and Nick to stop laughing. Eventually they did.

'Right then, we are going to have to shoogle,' said Nick, 'and get Malc.'

The first time Stefan had heard the word 'shoogle' was when he was visiting Mamo with Malc. Malc laughed and told him it meant to move or wobble. Mamo had meant it was time for them to go. They had taken the hint and went. It then became a word they often used at home.

Stefan laughed at the thought of himself shoogling ever again.

'It will have to be you,' he said to Nick. 'My ankle hurts too much. You get Malc and tell him all about the scary giants!'

The next few minutes went by in a blur. There was so much running around, it made Stefan feel even dizzier.

Chapter Eight

Malc came running with Nick, only to discover what he had been told was true. He then ran back to the camp to tell everyone the good news.

All the men then came running, and they in turn discovered it was true. There were no giants. There never had been any giants. Christmas was safe. Then they ran and told the IBs and everyone in The-Front-of-Beyond.

Then Mor turned up with Mamo behind her. She fussed in her usual way but smiled a lot too. Mamo said everyone should have cake.

Beyonders burst out of their doors, and happy children followed them. Everyone ran towards Giant's Hill to find out for themselves. It was true. Everyone began to cheer, clap and dance. They danced on their own shadows. They danced around the trolls. What a glorious, happy day it was. Everyone danced until they could dance no more.

The IBs each patted Stefan's head in turn and shook his hand. The best thing was when Malc heaved him up onto his shoulders. As he did so, Malc whispered into Stefan's ear,

'You are a hero.'

It was good.

Just like Nelson.

Chapter nine

A few days later, Stefan found himself standing in the school hall. It was the end of term assembly, and all the children were there. He had been given the rest of the week off school to rest and put his ankle up, which fortunately wasn't broken. What was really good was that it had started to snow that morning as he walked to school.

Soft snowflakes had stroked his nose and chin as he walked. It made him think of Mor's gentle kiss at bedtime. It was a perfect start to a special day.

Today was the special Christmas assembly. All the children were excited. It was the custom for every child in the school to be given a small present of some sweets. Each present was wrapped in the Christmas paper they had made themselves out of papier-mâché.

A photographer would come to the school and take a photo of every child. The photos were then printed off, and each one would be handed his own photo, which they would then attach to the Christmas paper they had made. Then they had to hand them in to the teacher. The ladies from The-Front-of-Beyond would then come to the school, wrap the sweets up in the paper and stick the photos on the front.

Usually the head teacher, Miss Sit-up-straight, gave the sweets out at the Christmas assembly, but she had

Chapter nine

asked Stefan to do it instead because he was a brave Beyonder hero.

Stefan was now feeling a bit nervous. He had never stood at the front of the school hall before. The sight of six lines of children all sitting on the floor looking at him made him feel very special.

The teachers sat on chairs behind the children. At the very back of the hall were four lines of parents also sitting down. He spotted Mor in the centre of the first row with Mamo, who had been given pride of place as a senior citizen. It was a small village school, but Stefan felt he was standing in a football stadium. The Christmas day of presents was just as good as any football match.

Miss Sit-up-straight raised her hand.

'Now sit up straight, children.'

This was a signal for everyone to stop talking. They did so.

'Now, children, this is a very important day. As you all know, Stefan has been very brave, and now he is going to present you all with your Christmas sweets. He will read your name out one at a time. You will then collect your present and go back to where you were sitting. Do you all understand?'

'Yes, Miss Sit-up-straight,' all the children said together.

'Here you are then, Stefan.'

Miss Sit-up-straight then handed a bag of sweets to Stefan, and Stefan called the name of the child written on it. It was Jimmy Campbell. Jimmy came up and collected his sweets. Then it was the turn of a girl called Moira Anderson to do the same. It continued like that, boy then girl, until

The Christmas Hero

all the bags had been given out. Proud parents clapped enthusiastically, and lots of photographs were taken.

'Now, Stefan, it is your turn. Here is your present,' said Miss Sit-up-straight.

She handed him his present. Stefan said thank you, and everyone cheered.

'Now, Stefan, stay here as we have a surprise for you. An important gentleman from our village is here to give you something very special.'

A lot of oohs and aahs went around the hall. And with that, from the back of the hall came the Reverend Hard-pew. He walked to the front of the hall and turned around to face the children and parents.

The first thing Stefan noticed about the Reverend Hard-pew was that he had shaved off his beard. And he was smiling. Stefan thought the Reverend Hard-pew looked so much better without his beard. He had never seen the Reverend Hard-pew smile before either.

Stefan wondered if maybe it had been the Reverend Hard-pew's beard that stopped him from smiling! Maybe the hair near his lips tickled when he smiled. Stefan decided not to have a beard when he grew up as he liked smiling a lot.

The Reverend Hard-pew coughed. Everyone went very quiet, even the mothers at the back of the hall who had been making most of the noise. Stefan wondered what was coming next. He didn't have to wait long.

One of the teachers got up and walked out of the hall. She came back carrying a large parcel covered by a brown paper bag and handed it to Miss Sit-up-straight. Miss Sit-up-straight then handed it to the Reverend Hard-pew.

Chapter nine

Stefan noticed that Miss Sit-up-straight's face had gone bright pink. The Reverend Hard-pew turned to Stefan and said, 'Stefan Bell, I have the honour of presenting this award to you today. You are a credit to your carers, your school and above all to The-Front-of-Beyond. Without you, we may all be still living in fear.'

Everyone in the hall clapped and cheered.

The Reverend Hard-pew then took the cover off the mysterious package and handed it to Stefan.

Stefan looked at it and gasped. It was a silver cup with these words engraved on it: 'To Stefan Bell, in honour of a selfless act bravely done.'

There was even more clapping and cheering.

'And it wouldn't be The-Front-of-Beyond if there wasn't a cake,' added the Reverend Hard-pew.

Everyone laughed.

The Reverend Hard-pew then nodded to Miss Sit-up-straight, who went pink again. She then nodded to the teacher who had brought the cup in. The teacher got up and went out, returning with a dinner trolley which was covered with a white tea cloth. She wheeled the trolley to the front of the hall to where Stefan was standing and whisked the cloth off.

Stefan was amazed. It was a cake above all others. The cake had been covered in white icing, and on top of it in golden icing was David killing Goliath. The detail was magnificent, even the sling and stone in David's hand were there. He looked at it speechless with happiness and pride.

The Reverend Hard-pew then shook Stefan's hand.

Stefan managed a whispered thank you. He was glad he wasn't expected to make a speech. He would have struggled to find any words to say.

The Reverend Hard-pew had more to say. 'And also, children, we must not forget Nick. He played an important part in all of this in looking after his brother. Nick, please come to the front.'

Stefan watched Nick get out of his seat and walk to where the Reverend Hard-pew was standing. Stefan grinned at him as he came near. Nick grinned back.

'Nick Bell, we are all proud of you.'

The Reverend Hard-pew then took an envelope out of his pocket and gave it to Nick.

Everyone clapped again.

'You can look in the envelope,' said the Reverend Hard-pew.

Nick did so. The look on his face said it all. He managed a faint thank you, then looked down at his feet.

Stefan learned later that day that Nick had been given a ticket to see his favourite football team play as well as fifty pounds to spend.

Miss Sit-up-straight, who had moved to one side of the hall when the cake was being wheeled in, now walked to where the Reverend Hard-pew was standing. She was very pink now. Stefan wondered if she was getting the chicken pox. He had been very pink when he'd had the chicken pox!

She gave a little cough.

'Now, children, the Reverend Hard-pew is going to tell you all a story. Stefan and Nick, you sit down with your class. You can leave your presents on the trolley.'

They did so.

Chapter nine

Miss Sit-up-straight waited until they had sat down, then moved to a vacant chair at the side of the hall and sat on it.

'Thank you, Miss Sit-up-straight,' said the Reverend Hard-pew. 'Now, everyone, I am going to tell you the beginning of a story. This is a true story about a special baby who came to the world to save us from all the bad things we do. His name is Jesus.

'One day a lady called Mary was visited by an angel called Gabriel. The angel said, "Don't be afraid, because God is pleased with you. You will have a special baby who will be great, and you will call him Jesus. He will be God's own Son." Mary lived in a place called Nazareth, and she was going to marry a man called Joseph.

'Joseph was worried when he found out that Mary was going to have a baby, but an angel came to him in a dream. The angel said, "Don't be frightened, Joseph, because God has chosen Mary to be the mother of his Son. It is alright to marry her."

'Now in those days, the Roman emperor who was in charge wanted to have a list of all the people in the different cities and towns to make sure they paid their taxes. He ordered that everyone had to go back to the towns where their families came from. They had to write their names in a register.

'This meant that Mary and Joseph had to travel from Nazareth to a town called Bethlehem, because that was where Joseph's family came from. Lots of people walked, but some people had donkeys to ride on. It was a long way to go, and Mary must have felt very tired. She knew that her baby would be born soon.

'When Mary and Joseph arrived at Bethlehem, it was full of people who had come to sign the register. They needed somewhere to stay, but there were no vacancies at the inns. Everywhere was full up. Mary and Joseph must have been very worried . They were far from home. Would they find anywhere for Mary to have her baby? What do you think, children?'

Then the Reverend Hard-pew stopped speaking. Everyone was silent. Stefan wanted the Reverend Hard-pew to carry on. He wanted to hear the end of the story.

'Now, children, I can see by your faces you all want to hear the end of the story. Well, to find out, I want you all to come to church on Christmas Day.'

Stefan heard lots of yeses behind him.

Stefan thought about the story he had just heard. He had saved his village from giants that turned out not to be real. He felt good about that, and getting a cup with his name on it was fantastic. He was glad that Nick had got a special present too.

But he had learned something more important than saving the village from giants. He had learned that true heroes always tell the truth.

And now, hearing the story of Jesus who could save everyone from all the bad things in the world—this just had to be the best thing ever. He couldn't wait until Christmas Day to hear the rest of the story.

This was really good, better than Nelson.

The End

The rest of the story about Jesus being born is in the Bible, Matthew 1–2 and Luke 1–2.